MW01269293

The Black and White of Truth

MELISSA M. GARRETT

This book is dedicated to RorryII, Thaddaeus, Amber, Nicole, Sherrice, and Kassidy. May you seek and obtain great levels of joy and abundance in every area of your life…for it is yours to have.

"Every human being's essential nature is perfect and faultless, but after years of immersion in the world, we easily forget our roots and take on a counterfeit nature."

Lao-tzu

The thief comes only in order to steal and kill and destroy. I came that they may have and enjoy life, and have it in abundance (to the full, till it overflows).

John 10:10, Amplified Bible (AMP)

Never go against yourself because you know YOU better than anyone else; be true to your own self.

Thanks, Mary these words will forever live in my heart, mind, and soul.

Roy Sr., thank you for protecting me as my purpose emerged!

Table of Contents

Introduction

"Most of the shadows of this life are caused by our standing in our own sunshine." — Ralph Waldo Emerson

The Black and White of Truth is based on the premise that every person can have a life of abundance in Health, Wealth, Relationships, and Service to others if living in truth, without intentional harm toward others is a chief aim.

The Black and White of Truth wants to expose the source of the fear factor that binds us and gives us the illusion that something is impossible and conversely the courage factor that gives us the vision everything is possible. Another way to say it is: we want to uncover the thinking and habits that keep us from embracing who we are and allow our internal compass to guide our actions and expressions toward a life of purpose and satisfaction.

Lastly, while this book is classified as a self-help book it is not or intended to be a book of instruction-my goal with sharing this book is to provoke you to realize your internal truth. The truth is that we have the answers already-the challenge lies in our ability to hear ourselves.

The concepts discussed throughout the *Black and White of Truth* are all about the importance of knowing and believing in self and learning to leverage external inputs that hone our ability to better understand our purpose and power.

There will be many guides, teachers and examples throughout our lives from which we will grow and learn, but we must never replace the quest for our personal truth to mimic someone else's truth.

 **Chapter 1**

MOVING AWAY FROM THE GRAY

"Earth is crammed with Heaven and every common bush is afire with God. But only he who sees takes off his shoes." -E.B. Browning

Truth requires us to respond to the black-and-white circumstances in life and not create gray as distractions. Gray is the result of mixing the pros and cons of black-and-white facts in an attempt to find an alternative to what is reality. It can also occur when we include non-related factors to create justification ("just fiction") to mask our inability to address the facts.

The phrase "black and white" represents "one idea that is clearly right and another that is clearly wrong, so that it is not difficult for you to make a moral decision. — Macmillan English Dictionary

The color gray is between black and white and is often used to describe lack of clarity; it has even been referred to in weather forecasts as cloudy or lack of brightness from the sun.

"Living in the gray" means not embracing truth as a starting point for all other decisions and actions. Gray is symbolic for mixing truths, which eventually results in something that is neither right nor wrong, neither up nor down, neither good nor bad. You get the point; it is basically a false reality that we just hang out in with a numbness that is sometimes powerless and more often unfulfilling.

The reason we create and accept this state of being is often a result of external influences. When we allow external influences to dictate who we are without regard to our internal compass, we set ourselves up for disappointment and unfulfilled lives. The energy and power of disappointment and lack of fulfillment can only yield depression, oppression, and more expressions of lack.

The goal of moving from the gray of life to acknowledging the black and white of self-truth and our divine right will make the difference in how much peace, joy, and abundance we will create, experience, and give in a lifetime.

Our truth can guide us both consciously and subconsciously; unfortunately what we call truth may or may not give us a good feeling or scenario, but it is a necessary starting point for taking control of our lives. The first step in improving anything is to understand the current state of affairs; only then can improvement be realized and appreciated.

If reality is not pleasing to us, then we should begin the process of changing the scenario. You may be thinking, "What is the difference with this approach versus the 'fake it until you make it' or other coping mechanisms?" There is a great difference in deciding to focus on the root or source of a circumstance versus responding and accepting circumstances we dislike in a defeating manner. For example, if every time you are preparing for work, you become anxious and unhappy — but you tell yourself that you need the money, and you should be grateful to have a job in this day and age. O.K., all these things may be true statements, but the fact remains that there is something giving you a signal through discomfort about your job or the process of going to your job. I am suggesting that perhaps you first accept the fact that there is something that needs further consideration from you, even if you conclude that you don't like your job but determine that there aren't any immediate options.

Starting with the truth versus denying your internal signals will allow you to begin to affect the change necessary and address the scenarios related to the source of your anxious and unhappy emotions when preparing to go to work. The key in this example is to begin with truth and seek the answer to that truth, instead of solving for something completely unrelated-like I don't like to get up early or I dread the traffic. The truth of the matter is these are nice distractions that dilute the black and white truth and push us into accepting less joy, peace and purpose in life-otherwise known as living in the gray.

Sowing our energy into the activities required to make changes to the areas of our lives we are not content with is the first step in taking responsibility for our destiny — instead of continuing to busy ourselves with distractions of guilt, false humility, and self-depriving chatter that only keep us in a holding pattern. We can begin to leverage the power of creativity to encourage and promote the personal determination necessary to experience the life we want and deserve.

Can you imagine anything sadder and more unrewarding than spending your lifetime living according to expectations, dreams, visions, and goals that originate and belong to someone else? There are two things wrong with this picture, the first is what we don't use of ourselves doesn't get shared with the world, and the second is that we cannot duplicate the contribution of someone else. So basically there is no value in suppressing who we are to mimic the contribution that can only be made by another. The other trap is giving in to the expectations of others or creating expectations of others versus allowing ourselves and others the freedom to be and do what comes naturally in our desires.

We often are looking for a reason not to trust ourselves, even to the point of creating obstacles or viewing obstacles as insurmountable. The fact of the matter is we must develop and trust that everything we need to live a life of satisfaction, inclusive of peace, love, joy, and abundance--is within us; we also have enough within us to give productively and positively to the lives of others in a meaningful way.

The ability to trust ourselves and overcome the fear of being in control of our own destiny is a complex proposition. The complexity is tied to the many false truths we have adopted through tradition, religion, relationships, and self-denial. These false truths create the illusion of impossibilities. They lead us to believe that our ability to obtain or experience certain goals or outcomes is based on something other than a decision to attract these things into our lives. Yes, depending on what truths we have accepted, the process may take longer or pose different routes to completion, but in the end all is possible. An important consideration is to make sure we start with our authentic self, because self will guide us to our appropriate truth.

It is when we begin to go after the dreams and aspirations that originate from others that we find ourselves on a journey to frustration. The frustration comes from the notion that something we desire is out of our reach. So we frustrate ourselves by magnifying the obstacles to minimize the ache of not satisfying the desire. It's like trying to unlock a door of opportunity with the wrong key! If this happens to us, then perhaps we have the keys to someone else's locked door or maybe we have locked our door with fear. If the belongs to someone else then give it back to them if you have locked yourself out from fear, generally we must step back and make sure we are clear about our motives and that we are at the right door for the opportunity we are seeking.

We hold the key to every fear-locked door in the pockets of our inner self. The journey is determining which doors we want to open, and then developing the knowledge, determination, and courage to reach inside ourselves and locate the key that will unlock any door of possibility we desire. We will begin to see that some doors don't require a key; they just require the wisdom to knock, and the door to our desires will be opened.

The metaphor "locked door" is used because it symbolizes the entrance to the unknown or the entrance to great thought-out expectations. In either case it is movement toward or away from something. When we walk up to a door, we expect to walk through it to gain access to something or someone that is the objective of our visit. The first step is to determine what it is that we are aiming for, so we can find the right door. The second step is to open the door and gain access to what is behind the door; and the last step is to walk through the door, make a connection, and obtain the objective of our visit.

Trusting the directions that lead us to a door without certainty about what is behind a door when visiting somewhere for the first time is very symbolic of how our internal truth guides us based on what we desire. We follow our internal persuasion with full expectation that what we will encounter the objects of our affections and purpose. When we can do this as easily as we trust our GPS navigation systems-then we will begin to understand the power of our internal truth.

The conditions of the door and the name on or above the door are signs and descriptors of what is potentially behind a door. For example, if you wanted to buy a book and walked up to a door where the sign read "Auto Shop," you would not expect to find books for sale.

Then why is it that so many of us say we are expecting to obtain one thing, but we stand outside of a door where the sign clearly indicates that what we desire is not likely to be accessible in that location?

What about those of us who have our expectations clearly defined—we have the address to the location and maybe even have done a drive-by to make sure we have the right address—but for some reason we can't knock on the door?

What about having a list of clearly documented objectives and the directions to the door location, but we've knocked on the door and no one answers?

OK, one more: What if we have a list of clearly documented objectives and an address and directions to the door, but we've knocked on the door and no one answers—and we notice a sign that says "Come on in," yet when we turn the handle, the door will not open?

These are four examples of the way obstacles materialize in our thoughts as well as how external situations and circumstances play a part in helping us explain away the beliefs that we treasure and truly value. These are the times when living in the gray is more appealing than challenging truths that seem impossible or may create more pain than reward.

In example one, knowledge and clarity of goals may be the root cause for why there is an obvious disconnect between our proclaimed desires and our actions. The second scenario demonstrates zeal to plan and gain knowledge, but a fear of failure creates blockage. The satisfaction of knowing may override actual attainment. In the third example, clarity of goals, planning, and knowledge is followed by an empty demonstration of expectation, which is a destructive energy against positive hopes and ideas. The last example is when some of the most determined individuals meet their final test of expectation, and fail.

The five senses kick in and cause us to begin importing logic to explain the unexplainable power of faith and expectation, which create reality. Again, I submit to you that the door is not locked — it is our beliefs and fears that lock doors or create obstacles for entry. In either case, further probing for instruction and direction is suggested versus retreating to logic of defeat. Remember, faith without works or action is dead or of no result. Work or action could be to be still and listen for instructions from our small internal voice of truth- which can take more effort than building a concrete bridge.

 **Chapter 2**

The KEY <small>(Know that Each thought You think)</small> CREATES TRUTH

"If what we sow is what we reap, then how can our fate be anything other than what we have sown in words, deeds, or thoughts?"

– M. Garrett

There are many debates among religious beliefs, sects, and cults, as well as the possible intersections between science and religion, and one could easily spend a lifetime defending and defining a position of personal preference without ever experiencing the proclaimed benefits of any specific belief.

The Black and White of Truth challenges us to turn our efforts from living in the grayness of life—defending and defining a belief—to seeking out and experiencing the truth within a belief. More simply put, if we believe in something and we are not experiencing what that belief proclaims, should we accept the gap through justification, or should we be determined to realize the results of our proclaimed belief?

The Black and White of Truth is not focused on defending or promoting the viewpoint of a specific belief, sector, or cult; instead it is about inspiring us to take personal responsibility for the condition of our lives. Yes, I am saying that whatever our personal preference (Scientologist, atheist, vagabond, elitist, Christian, Catholic, Greek Orthodox, Angelical, Reformed, Restoration, Muslim, Jewish, Rastafarian, Buddhist, Hindu, Confucian, Native American, Polynesian, spiritualist, Mormon, Jehovah's Witness, Christian Science, and the list goes on), the choice to accept and believe in an established set of goals, objectives, and outcomes is ours to decide and achieve.

There is one common factor that applies across any sector, religion, or science, and that is the requirement to accept and believe in a central theme. In religious studies, developing faith is the critical initiation into a view of the world and how one should behave in it; in science it is developing consistent results to determine the probable behaviours and outcomes of some combination of items.

In most cases, these belief systems, including those handed down as tradition, are generally perceived as advantageous and necessary guidelines for how we live our lives. If this is not a true statement for you, then please keep reading in the hope that there will be something included in this writing that will inspire you to evaluate why you would accept and believe in anything that is destructive to you. On the other hand, if you have accepted and believe in living your life according to principles that aim you toward improving and enhancing your life, *The Black and White of Truth* will help you expedite or improve the grasp of those desired goals, objectives, and outcomes—especially those that you have not been able to achieve.

The objective of this chapter is to set the captives free from believing that anyone other than us has power over the quality of our lives and our individual destinies. We did not create ourselves, but we do make our lives through what we believe, accept, and do with our mind, body, and spirit.

And Jesus said unto them, Because of your unbelief: for verily I say unto you, if ye have faith as a grain of mustard seed, ye shall say unto this mountain, Remove hence to yonder place; and it shall remove; and nothing shall be impossible unto you. (Matthew 17:20 KJV)

Please note, the concepts being shared are related to how we govern our lives and not the lives of others. How we decide to respond to a situation or what we accept in our lives has nothing to do with the actions of others. So as you continue to read, remove what you think others need to do from your mind's picture and focus on what and how you can improve your state of living. It will amaze you to see how over time the level of importance or impact that you once believed someone else contributed to your life has either decreased or ceased to exist. As you begin to take personal accountability for your life and what you are expecting for your future, it will become apparent that freedom is created from within us.

Accept the fact that abundant health, wealth, relationships, and service are a natural law of the universe, and thought is the active principle by which we are related to those things we need and desire. Thought equals mind in action, producing through creative energy, so knowing this makes it impossible to blame someone else for our fate. It is our faith and belief system that is responsible for what we experience.

For some, the first major step is to realize that abundant health, wealth, relationships, and service are possible life experiences and not accept the lie that life is a deck of cards and you just did not get any aces. Instead-continue to seek out new decks, dealers and games until you create a winning game hand.

For many, the first step is to go beyond accepting the truth to actually experiencing abundant health, wealth, relationships, and service without falling into the trap of believing that because we are better off than many that somehow we should be content. Gratitude is always right, but don't use it as a crutch to minimize what you can be grateful about.

For the few, who already believe and experience a life of abundant health and wealth, and through relationships and service. The opportunity for us is to continue to reach out and encourage others to experience the same for themselves. There is no end to abundance; therefore there is enough to go around. So to not share and care about the enlightenment of would be oppressive and selfish.

Just a quick observation: there will always be those who will not embrace the possibilities discussed in this book-our responsibility is to share not dictate or judge.

Understanding how our words shape our lives is sometimes the hardest concept to convey. There are so many documentaries and books based on research and consistent observations that demonstrate how our words can work for us or work against us. This is exactly the point in which we must understand the importance of our inner truth. If we say one thing with our voice, but our innermost desires are of some other belief, we instantly create a conflict that will either bless us or curse us. This is why so many people have become skeptical and frustrated with these principles. There are always at least two communication streams in process: one, our conscious and verbal expectations, and two, our subconscious and most often overlooked inner expectations.

The opportunity is in bringing these two communication streams into alignment, thereby creating our environment. As always people like to debate which communication stream is more powerful or more controlling. I'm not joining the debate over which comes first or which is more powerful because the fact of the matter is that both conscious thinking and subconscious knowing must be aligned.

Spoken, conscious words can persuade the inner voice over time and vice versa. That's why it is so important to acknowledge and understand what our inner self is sharing. If what is coming out of our inner self is not prosperous to us and others, then we must begin to use our spoken words to persuade differently. The key is that we must start with our truth and then work to improve ourselves toward a divine truth. What divine truth? I'm glad you asked. It is the right of each living being to have life and have it more abundantly. This is the black and white of truth: "yes" to abundance and "no" to anything else!

Chapter 3

KNOWLEDGE TO REACH INSIDE OF SELF

My people perish because of a lack of knowledge. — Hosea 4:6

This chapter is about the process to move from concept to preparation. Many people I speak with share their knowledge and desires of experiencing a life of abundant health, wealth, relationships, and service in great detail with very convincing passion and much conviction, yet there is no real manifestation to support their desires. I've found that an important piece is missing for actualization, and it has to do with their belief or expectation that these gifts are available for them.

To experience the desires of our heart, we have to not only believe that something is possible, but we have to believe that that something is possible *for us*. Many use visualization exercises to help with this stage of transformational thinking. I suggest a concept called the "Z" Vision Board (see the illustration):

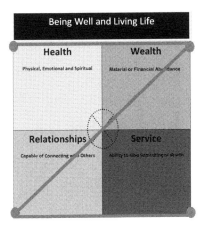

The "Z" vision board concept is a practical way to organize and connect the activities and objectives for the primary areas of our life. The "Z" pattern is not concerned with what is in each quadrant but rather helps the author prioritize efforts and maximize their experiences.

Use the "Z" Board to identify and understand certain desires that resonate from within. This is similar to traditional vision board exercises: find the items, pictures, words, and symbols that illustrate your goals and objectives. The discipline is in organizing the expectations. Organization of goals and desires is not to be confused with determining the channel or way in which they will be accomplished. The focus of the exercise is to get a mental and emotional picture of what you are saying you want to accomplish.

This exercise is not magic, but it is a proven method for starting the process of acceptance, which is followed by positive affirmations that serve to transform thinking and habits that may be obstacles to achieving certain desires. The age old principle Law of Attraction tells us to focus on what we want versus what we don't want. For example, if you want financial abundance, don't spend your energy focusing on financial lack. Remember, we attract what we think about, talk about and fear. Another important point is to understand the role of obstacles. They exist as we perceive them, but the most troublesome obstacles are the ones that are almost undetectable.

Obstacles are not the big bad things we often struggle to remove, they are the "ankle biters" that we don't even notice. One of the most elusive obstacles is the inability to hear and receive the truth and guidance required to actually accomplish a goal or desire. If we can conceive a thought, then it is a possibility. Possibility requires some level of effort, knowledge, or acceptance to be made a reality. How many of these ingredients will be based on our individual circumstances and our ability to believe in our personal power to leverage the universal power?

For example, a focus on improving the mind, body, and spirit is essential for abundant health, which provides the energy and wisdom to accumulate financial increase and material belongings in support of financial abundance. The energy, wisdom, financial increase, and material belongings derived from abundant health and wealth are void without someone to share them with, and that's where relationships and service are magnified. Notice, I said "magnified" because our health and wealth are always tied to relationships and service at some level.

The magnification comes from the freedom to give when we are not consumed with lack of balance mentally, physically, and spiritually, or financially and materially. I know you are thinking, "What if I am content with not having abundant health and wealth and would rather build relationships and give what I can to service?" I would not disagree with your decision, but I would ask, "Why not magnify what you can contribute to both those you are in a relationship with as well as those you desire to give service to? The answer is easy for me: if we accept lack for ourselves, then we certainly will not see the fallacy in giving less to others as a disservice since it is seemingly our best.

Our conviction that the content of our faith or belief system is true becomes the basis of our existence. We can know many things, but until we develop a conviction that it is truth, it is just knowledge. This divide between knowledge and truth serves us well, since we would not want to inadvertently accept certain truths without some level of personal contemplation and acceptance.

As we are exposed to various teachings or experiences, we gain knowledge and preference toward a belief system. As that knowledge increases either voluntarily or involuntarily, our conviction strengthens, and eventually we become reliant on that belief system. In other words we believe, and through our knowledge of these principles, we begin to expect a certain outcome.

Personal trust and reliance occurs when our expectations outweigh our doubts. Doubts are minimized or eliminated when we are awakened to the truth from acquiring knowledge voluntarily or involuntarily.

As discussed earlier, we have accepted, embraced, and adopted so many mixed truths that we find living in the gray a much easier proposition than seeking and experiencing real truth. Moving from the grayness of a mediocre-at-best life requires us to use our words to form our life starting with the Black and White of Truth.

 **Chapter 4**

WISDOM TO TRUST OURSELVES

"Increase in me that wisdom that discovers my true interest. Strengthen my resolution to perform what that wisdom dictates." – Benjamin Franklin

In this chapter we will explore the principles behind leveraging the knowledge from the previous chapters to move from preparation into action. Having high expectations from the wrong information can be very dangerous and very disappointing.

We all have the ability to think, but it is what and how we think that influences the results and outcomes. Knowledge serves as a catalyst to bring wisdom into effect. Wisdom requires knowledge; unfortunately many of us have tapped into knowledge without obtaining the required wisdom to create the expected results.

Wisdom brings just judgment or insight with knowledge. Just judgment and insight speak to personal experience and personal alignment. In other words there is more involved than stating facts. There is some resolve and deep-rooted conviction required to activate creation and manifestation.

Others can provide us with lots of knowledge about many topics, but it isn't until we merge our insight and personal experience with their knowledge that we can generate wisdom.

The key in the pocket of our inner self is the realization of the power of thoughts and words, which will unlock every seemingly locked door. It's not knowing, not believing, not transforming our thought pattern, not changing our actions and not having the right expectations that allow us to stand in front of a door with the key in our pocket able to unlock abundant health, wealth, relationships, and service and not use it.

"Our ultimate struggle is not with each other, or with theological or humanistic systems of thought (as different as they may be), or even flesh and blood, but with principalities and powers." Contrary to popular belief, it is not all about us. *The Game of Life and How to Play It.* by Florence Scovel Shinn

FOR OUR STRUGGLE IS NOT AGAINST FLESH AND BLOOD, BUT AGAINST THE RULERS, AGAINST THE AUTHORITIES, AGAINST THE POWERS OF THIS DARK WORLD AND AGAINST THE SPIRITUAL FORCES OF EVIL IN THE HEAVENLY REALMS. (Ephesians 6:12)

It is the comfort we find in gravitating toward the gray areas of life that creates the struggle within us. When logic can't take us any further, it is then time to hold onto our inner truth and kindly or forcibly move our ego out of the way. Focusing on differences in opinions, approach, and belief systems—also known as living in the gray-- is just a distraction from honing in on the real power that will attract and create a life that is abundant in health, wealth, relationships, and service to others.

We must allow ourselves to know and trust the original truth that was good and pleasing, and not allow our ego to step in and save the day or, should I say, push us to the gray where there is familiarity.

Ego's job is to protect us and our perception of truth. In case I didn't mention it, ego is *all* about *us* and not the good of the whole as we tend to reason. What something feels like to us, what we hear that affects us, and what we should say to protect ourselves or those things we believe belong to us. The fact of the matter is that any productive truth we start with will not only benefit us but also many others around us. This is a good litmus test to use when evaluating whether we are dealing with a black or white truth or a modified gray truth, originating from our ego or popular influence.

Ego is the primary orchestrator of division and strife. Conversely, it is humility that fosters respect and compassion toward others. It is our ego that we spend years of early life developing and shaping into a perspective that challenges our real self. The unfortunate truth is that we spend a great deal of our lifetime becoming something other than ourselves and then the remaining years trying to get back to what we were originally. I'm not suggesting that we sacrifice our own peace, joy, and happiness for the sake of others. I am, however, emphasizing the importance of understanding the true source of our peace, joy, and happiness.

Learning to hear ourselves is a critical starting point. For example, we wouldn't have a fair chance at winning a race if we didn't hear the instructions to start running or if we ran in the wrong direction. This is why we sometimes feel out of the game and hopeless: because we start with the wrong instructions. Wrong instructions take on many forms: our upbringing, our understanding of certain religious customs, our need to please others, and the list goes on.

Starting with our inner truth, whatever it may be is a better place over the long haul. In the short term, many of us can pull off covering up our true identity and desires, and unfortunately some of us can get lost during the cover-up process. Losing sight of who we are, is tragic and a waste of a good life of contribution.

We are original individuals with unique thoughts; even when we agree with others, we are bringing something different to the table. Now let's not confuse this concept with that of being a rebel in training versus learning to trust ourselves enough to embrace our truths as a baseline for everyday interactions and future planning.

Getting advice from someone in an area of his or her expertise or experience can be a wise proposition. Accepting conflicting advice regarding our internal desires causes us to move into areas of gray. This often occurs when we mix our Black and White of Truth with the black and white of someone else's truth.

It is in a state of humility that we can let go of what we have been taught through words, deeds, observations, expectations, and experiences to take hold of what it is we truly desire and are subconsciously seeking. It is certainly easier said than done, because we have inherently developed and accepted new truths. Some of these truths are inspiring and encouraging, while others are limiting and binding. It is our responsibility to evaluate our belief system and the results of the principles behind our beliefs to ensure that we are aligned with our innermost desires and that the alignment is bringing us the most abundant and joyous life we can experience.

I've expressed the importance of acknowledging our personal truth, of gaining knowledge to motivate, but it is only our internal wisdom that will propel us into the divine truth.

 Chapter **5**

DETERMINATION TO UNLOCK TRUTH

"The same power that binds is the power that releases."
– unknown

Sometimes we can seemingly have all the pieces but can't fit the puzzle together. That's when determination becomes the catalyst for results. There is a popular saying that "Rome wasn't built in a day." Similarly our thought patterns and internalized beliefs are a result of some consistent personal patterns and experiences that could benefit from a different perspective to foster more and different thoughts of possibilities, where previous limiting thoughts and small expectations once resided. This is a process, but no change is beyond our ability.

To transform legacy and traditional thought patterns requires a high level of deliberate and focused thinking to point to new possibilities and not old experiences. Many believe that experience is the best teacher, but sometimes it can be the largest roadblock to better ideas and experiences.

That's why determination is so critical in staying the course for creating transformational thinking. Knowing what to do is no match for the wisdom of execution. Being determined to experience a particular outcome requires that vision to be held in place by any means necessary.

Since we don't know when our revelation of wisdom will become sufficient enough to produce manifestation of our divine truth, we must be determined to stay focused and true to our thoughts of the Black and White of Truth.

Keeping the gray out requires us to press our way into a higher place of expectation while we wait. Some will call it faith; others may call it the realm of possibility. In either case we are convinced of something unseen. Often we are OK with this phase until others begin to ask questions and sway us toward doubt and the gray, indicating it's time to justify the possibilities of gray versus believing and accepting the Black and White of Truth that we can have the life we want.

Again, the principle of accepting black and white truth is not about wishing really hard. And yes, obtaining certain goals may require working through defined processes.

The emphasis is not on something magically happening. The energy to believe and expect is what releases the required people, process, connections, and resources we need to create the lives we desire. If we can perceive a thing in our conscious minds and hold it in our subconscious mind, then we will have the courage and resolve to do the things necessary to obtain it.

The obstacle to our resolve often comes from fear or lack of knowledge, but if our inner self is determined, then we can attract the necessary external support to fuel our internal desire. Remember, if we start with our truth, not the truth of someone else, this will work — regardless of how many times fear causes us to give up.

If we are starting with someone else's truth or expectation, it may be very hard to find the resolve to keep going when the appearance of opposition appears. This is because we have an external force that is not being met with equal resistance from within us. Most often this is described as lack of motivation, intimidation, depression, and fear of failure — all false realities from living in the gray.

This is where the rubber meets the road, so following are some affirmations and pointers to encourage us while we are waiting, better described as the creation and manifestation phase in which we must press our way toward our goals.

The Press...

While we wait, fear and panic cause us to work harder than necessary. The key to managing our level of fear is to use our energy wisely: knowing what to expect and knowing what to accept, knowing and reminding ourselves of our portion of divine truth, acting like an attorney by looking for rights and loopholes to our egotistic logic. After all, we are created beings, but we make ourselves. Another great waiting tactic is to call those things that are not as though they were: know how to use our words, our personal wills, and our voices. There is always an internal or external voice asking us why our words are not producing the results we proclaim and want to achieve.

The answer to this is very simple. If we believe our words, accept our words as truth, behave as our words proclaim, persuade our doubts to become truth, and finally rely on our internal truth to be the origin of our goals, we will create the environment we desire and deserve. The hard part of this process for many to grasp is the necessary alignment of spirit, mind, and body.

We cannot say one thing and believe another and expect it to manifest. We can, however, say one thing and what we believe manifests. How is this so? Because the entire process is based on getting our divine truth to manifest, and if our divine truth is not accurate, the way to change it is through our words and actions and not the other way around. That's why we start with knowledge of our divine rights and truth to understand just how much work is required to get our mind, body, and spirit aligned.

We've talked about how knowledge without wisdom is pretty ineffective. That's why it is so important to for us to learn how to stay motivated and inspired by truth. Sometimes this will require obtaining or reiterating certain knowledge, exposing ourselves to gifted and great teachings, and trusting ourselves to know which truth is our truth.

So many people are closed in and fearful of allowing themselves to hear new information because they believe that it will cause them confusion and in some cases harm. Well, it does feel uncomfortable to awaken a part of ourselves that has been sleeping for a long time. Some of my most painful moments have been realizing how complicated I made my life by deferring or denying the validity of certain personal truths, only to find out later that I had the answers and instructions all along my treacherous journey to gray and back to black or white.

What does this journey look like? It will be different for each of us, depending on our previous experiences, upbringing, cultural norms, and educational and socioeconomic exposure. However, the fact remains that we each have the same opportunity to live out our divine truths; the aforementioned items are just elements of gray that are often used to dismiss the possibility of divine truth. We just have to be determined to not be distracted. The process is sustained by remaining motivated and inspired to realize our divine truths. There are generally four essential aspects to self-motivation and inspiration that we will need to pay close attention to: our beliefs, convictions, attitude, and reliance.

Beliefs

Be not overwhelmed by the magnitude of some of our divine truths by remembering that we ourselves have everything we need to request and experience miracles.

Conviction

Who against hope believed in hope? Remember it is not what we see but what we know; it is being steadfast and being strong in faith and unwavering.

Attitude

Being fully persuaded by our choice to embrace divine truth, which gives us the stamina to press on and expect the results of divine truth.

Reliance

If we want to press toward the mark for the high calling of our divine truth, we must know how to keep our minds focused on high and heavenly places, which is where the work of the subconscious mind comes into play and embraces our desires until our logical or conscious senses can realize the divine truth.

Remember, it is a process!

 Chapter **6**

POWER TO EXPECT AND ACCEPT TRUTH

Not by might, nor by power, but by My Spirit. – Zechariah 4:6

The power is a childlike logic, absent of the fear and control that we have conditioned ourselves to accept as truth. We have grown so much in knowledge that we learn a great deal toward expecting manifestation as a result of much effort and toil. Sometimes we dismiss the power of childlike innocence, because we are looking for huge and complex solutions and circumstances.

Complexity is not a prerequisite for divine truth. As a matter of fact, accepting the laws of nature that we see in effect all day, everyday should be the simplest truth to accept. Divine truth is black and white. For example, abundance is available in every area of our lives, and anything else is not a truth we should accept.

Think back to when we were children, and we listened for hours to fairy tales that escaped all logic, but we were able to enjoy and experience the folly and magic being shared with us. We never questioned how a very large man could slide down a chimney half his size (even if we did not have a fireplace) to leave gifts for complete strangers. The details were not important, and even the most curious of the bunch was easily persuaded to continue the imaginative journey with just a gentle nudge.

The power to expect is similar to our childhood acceptance. We must work to embrace the black-and-white promises of truth, and not create a gray area to linger in because we neither accept nor believe divine truths. This is much more serious than a fairy tale; it is truly a matter of life and death. We can't merely hope and wish for our best life. Instead we must know and expect what belongs to us and how to use our power of expectation.

The knowing required happens in the inner self's wisdom, which comes from aligning our conscious knowledge and verbal proclamations with the truth of our subconscious self. Our spirit and soul are what gives life to our knowledgeable words.

"Knowledge speaks and wisdom listens." – unknown author

Expectations are only valid and honored when supported by the coming together of knowledge and wisdom. These critical intersections create the atmosphere for creating and attracting the life scenarios we accept as divine truths.

 Chapter 7

COURAGE TO EMBRACE THE TRUTH

"The only thing we have to fear is fear itself."
— Franklin D. Roosevelt

So often we find ourselves excited and determined about having desires or, in some cases, needs met, but for some reason we just can't muster up the strength to go after and capture the experience of actually obtaining.

I know this is shaky ground because there is a reluctance to push past the superficial belief that not having or wanting but still believing is somehow a great demonstration of faith.

It's quite comical to me how over time we have figured out how to not feel bad about feeling bad or how we intelligently explain away our own intellect-all in the name of the unexplainable. My favorite response has become silence in reverence to the omnipotent and omniscience of the universe.

Walking through the door of an expectation looks a lot like this in my mind: we determine a need or desire, we position our vision and heart towards it, we ask for it with words, and then we began the process of expectation. Sometimes this process is instantaneous, short, or unfolds over time; it just depends on what our life experience has taught us. I'm not criticizing or recommending any reward or penalty for the length of time it might take someone to grasp and receive his or her desires or needs. I would, however, like to assert the notion that while we are waiting, the goal is to increase expectations not secretly dismiss the request through self-created logic.

It's natural for our ego to take control in order to protect us. The ego is our biggest enemy during the times when we are expecting something perceived to be illogical.

"Sometimes we may have to forget what we were taught, so that we can remember what we know."
—*Wisdom of the Heart*, by Alan Cohen

Chapter 8

POSSIBILITIES OF THE TRUTH

"All things are possible to him who believes" — St. Mark 9:23

This chapter is not about socioeconomic or political motivations but rather the creation of curiosity about the possibilities that we can't necessarily frame up using our five senses. I'm referring to those things that must first be imagined and sketched out in our thoughts and then colored in, using our five senses. When we rely solely on our five senses, we are limiting our possibilities to only those things that currently exist. In doing this we shortchange our abundance and abandon the responsibility to be the captain of our lives, as well as diminish the service we give to those who have not realized how to live abundantly.

The previous chapters in this book are about how to remove the distractions that cause us to stand in front of great doors of possibilities and remain frustrated and intimidated by the locks, often becoming so occupied with the locks that we forget about the master key in our pockets.

We must not grow weary of unlocking possibilities for ourselves and others. Just think…if enough of this thinking was manifested, we would all in turn be a help to one another. I'm not suggesting a life of toil and unrest to the point of exhaustion or overzealous emphasis on accomplishing and obtaining stuff or even going out of our way to help every passerby. It's more about allowing ourselves to call forth the opportunities and possibilities that come naturally and our own innate abilities.

Each of us can be motivated by something different or can share the same values in principle. It is the sense of determination and degree of willingness that propels us into varying levels of action. Personally there can be some things that we just don't agree with but not to the point that we feel moved or inclined to exert the energy or resources to address. Then there are some global concerns that we instinctively believe can be harmful to ourselves, and perhaps a larger community over time, yet we somehow don't feel the need to get involved. These are both natural and typical responses to situations and circumstances.

The point here is to remind ourselves to not grow weary of being curious and interested in possibilities, because many times it is not about us but for someone else who will be inspired or motivated by our actions. When others are impacted by our resources, the Law of Reciprocity will repay us. This is not to say that we should be looking for a specific return on a specific deed, but be assured that there will be a return of similar kind.

Chapter 9

A Glimpse of My Truth Journey

"Mediocrity is a selfish sin." — M. Garrett

This isn't a magical journey; it will take some desire and discipline to get positive results. What this means is that we have to change our habits and thought patterns through creating a consistent flow of practices and information. To change and challenge the logic that our minds use today is not a small feat. As a matter of fact it must become a way of life in order to become real. I'm not suggesting that we will struggle to gain and then our successes will easily slip away, but I am saying that our ability to live and think in this new way of truth we must not forget that the same practices that pushed us into living in the gray and totally disregarding our truth is still in existence.

My journey is chocked full of wonderful examples of brilliance, stupidity, arrogance, humility, hurt, joy, pain, depression, elation and a list of ups and downs that could never be captured-even if I spent the next fifty years documenting them.

The point is that finding my personal truth was not an event. In fact the truth I found early on was that I must always listen and trust myself. In order to trust myself, I must learn to hear myself. This is where the fun begins...what the hell am I saying?-oh boy, I tried yoga, meditation, journaling, Jesus and so on. All very comforting, but as a result I slipped into an immediate state of depression. Why? Well, because, yoga revealed my physical inadequacies, meditation allowed me to hear my "crazy", Jesus caused me to develop a level of guilt that I can't even describe and I was so confused about my real thoughts I couldn't even enjoy journaling. Remember no judging me on whether I did something right or not-(this is my story).

So for me, with a sense of urgency I had to, put a lid on all my new findings to minimize the shock to my system from all this wonderful insight. I pursued this quest as if my very life depended on it-and it does.

In this relentless pursuit I began to stumble across books, poems, people and experiences like bread crumbs to a light source. If you are reading my story-it is not an accident-you were connected to this information because some part of you asked for it. Depending upon how strong or loud your voice is will dictate how you respond to this information.

I have been on this journey of truth for over fifteen years-so I realize that my readers will have various reactions ranging from indifference to "oh my" this is my missing piece. Wherever, you are in your journey, my hope is that you acknowledge your personal power and the rest will follow.

The good news is that as we make progress on this journey, we will not have to work so hard to convince our sub-conscious mind to accept our personal truths. We will expect greater outcomes versus self-prophecies of gloom and doom. To sustain our new thought patterns and personal results we will have to continuously fortify ourselves with healthy thoughts and practices that feed us emotional, spiritual and physical proof, that a life of abundance should be our experience. Maintaining a focus and determination to live abundantly is a lifelong quest.

Everyone will approach this journey in a slightly different manner, but there are some proven practices and key components. For example, reading and journaling for the mind, meditation for the spirit, exercise, and Yoga for physical endurance and being connected to like-minded individuals for inspiration and encouragement are critical elements for including our whole self in the transformation process-which by-the-way increases our success rate in obtaining our personal truths and sustaining our personal satisfaction.

My Favorite Poem for Reflection

The Journey by Mary Oliver

One day you finally knew
what you had to do, and began,
though the voices around you
kept shouting
their bad advice —
though the whole house
began to tremble
and you felt the old tug
at your ankles.
"Mend my life!"
each voice cried.
But you didn't stop.
You knew what you had to do,
though the wind pried
with its stiff fingers
at the very foundations,
though their melancholy
was terrible.
It was already late
enough, and a wild night,
and the road full of fallen
branches and stones.
But little by little,
as you left their voices behind,
the stars began to burn
through the sheets of clouds,
and there was a new voice
which you slowly
recognized as your own,
that kept you company
as you strode deeper and deeper
into the world,
determined to do
the only thing you could do —
determined to save
the only life you could save.

Suggested Books to Read

Key to Yourself, Venice Bloodworth

The Game of Life and How to Play it, Florence Scovel Shin

The Secret, Rhonda Byrne

The Method, Scott Soloff

The Four Agreements-Don Miguel Ruiz

Eat, Pray, Love, Elizabeth Gilbert

The Alchemist, Paulo Coelho

Excuses Begone!, Wayne W. Dyer

About the Author

Melissa M. Garrett is dedicated to sharing the knowledge and wisdom required to inspire others to expect a life abundant in health, wealth, relationships and service. She is founder and president of Conversations for Sisters, an outreach and personal development organization dedicated to empowering women of all ages to take control of their lives for the better. Melissa is a senior executive with over twenty-five years of experience in the strategic planning and implementation of large transformation programs. She is married with three children and resides in Aurora, Ohio.

"God created us, but we make ourselves." — Venice Bloodworth

Made in the USA
Middletown, DE
08 March 2024

50481912R00035